NEGRO MOUNTAIN

PHOENIX POETS

Edited by Srikanth Reddy

Rosa Alcalá, Douglas Kearney &

Katie Peterson, consulting editors

Negro Mountain

C. S. GISCOMBE

THE UNIVERSITY OF CHICAGO PRESS

CHICAGO & LONDON

The University of Chicago Press, Chicago 60637
The University of Chicago Press, Ltd., London
©2023 by The University of Chicago
Published 2023
Printed in the United States of America

32 31 30 29 28 27 26 25 24 23   1 2 3 4 5

ISBN-13: 978-0-226-82971-5 (paper)
ISBN-13: 978-0-226-82972-2 (e-book)
DOI: https://doi.org/10.7208/chicago/9780226829722.001.0001

Library of Congress Cataloging-in-Publication Data

Names: Giscombe, C. S., 1950- author.
Title: Negro Mountain / C. S. Giscombe.
Other titles: Phoenix poets.
Description: Chicago ; London : The University of Chicago Press, 2023. | Series: Phoenix poets |
    Includes bibliographical references.
Identifiers: LCCN 2023010344 | ISBN 9780226829715 (paperback) | ISBN 9780226829722 (ebook)
Subjects: LCSH: Negro Mountain (Pa. and Ma.)—Poetry | LCGFT: Poetry.
Classification: LCC PS3557.I78 N44 2023 | DDC 811/.54—dc23/eng/20230412
LC record available at https://lccn.loc.gov/2023010344

♾ This paper meets the requirements of ANSI/NISO Z39.48-1992 (Permanence of Paper).

CONTENTS

Negro Mountain was written in California—at 2534 Grant Street in Berkeley and in Room 2 of the National Hotel in Jamestown.

Portions of this book were composed in and near Bellefonte, Centre County, Pennsylvania.

Negro Mountain, in the Allegheny Range of the eastern United States, is a long ridge that straddles the Pennsylvania-Maryland border and the Mason-Dixon Line. The ridge has been known as Negro Mountain since the late eighteenth century because of "an incident" that took place there in the 1750s—in a skirmish between a band of English speculators, led by Thomas Cresap, and a party of Native Americans, a Black man accompanying the English group was killed by a shot fired by one of the Native Americans. The Black man's name (as it has been handed down in Pennsylvania stories) was Nemesis or Nemises. Brantz Mayer—in his 1851 book on the Iroquois leader Logan and the Cresap family—notes that "Negro Mountain [is] where a gigantic African who belonged to [Cresap's] party bequeathed his name in death to the towering cliffs."

The ridge's name, however, has been a matter of public controversy since the 1920s when the US Geological Survey declared Negro Mountain's highest point to be the highest point in the Commonwealth of Pennsylvania.

The Black man—called Nemesis or Nemises in the architecture of stories—who died on the ridge still called Negro Mountain is beyond reach. The mountain—the "very long shadow"—survives.

Seven Dreams

First Dream

Wolves came up the driveway and through the side yard of the old house—this

was in Kindergarten time—and I stood still though I was frightened

to be in their midst and they took note of me but did

not bite me or threaten me. The light was light I had known—by then—

having seen it in the hour before a thunderstorm: dull, bitter light and everywhere
   though

without apparent source. The wolves had ragged gray pelts—bad fur, tufts

of it—and their hindquarters were skinny in comparison to their very big shoulders.

They'd come in apparently from the street, Liscum Drive, and onto the property
   (which

was nearly an acre and had once been a farmstead), and they parted around where

I was standing. It was almost literally a wave of them, those wolves, as

though they'd come up the hill from West Third Street or somehow got through

the chain-link fence of the V.A. cemetery that traced the hill

on Liscum Drive.

A white friend wrote me, *the human figure passes through the animal*

pack unharmed. And she said that she saw the dream as being not about

the wolves as much as *passing through adversity*, this exchange

decades after the dream itself, which had been a thing of moment—visual, tinctured with obvious anxiety—current in my memory for that time before the

    year she

and I met.

      Make no mistake, dear and articulate friends, I knew it

was an unstable moment. My thumbs

were different, I'd seen, from one

another. Beyond the driveway had been pear and walnut trees.

One passes through a wood, or a track does.

A dull feeling overtakes you in the field.

There had been a gate at the driveway, but only

the posts remained, grown over by the hedges that stopped on either side

of the entrance from the street. What do hills

summarize? Origin stories? Right

and left separated long before this. Bait me, love

—I can pass until I speak.

Second Dream

I was a woman in a prison camp, my job

was to work in the yard. I walked away,

drifted north, like I do, and came to Canada; but by then I was

a man dressed in a long soviet coat, wool with a red collar. Better I

would have retreated to the mountains, I thought, or the interior.

Why not just go on *into* Canada? someone said.

It was how the border had appeared so quickly when my experience was

that the roads that were the way over were

always further north than I had figured when I'd set out.

In my experience—waking

life—nothing had readied me for such an arrival.

Walking north, I was surely out of bounds, a city woman, then

a man indistinguishable from his own prowess.

You know how I figure, I thought.

Typically, I dreamed and at the same time watched the dream.

The gate was open.

I watched myself as if from a car at a drive-in movie.

I could have been up on the angry mountains, I thought, that

could be the subject matter or the theme.

Someone else stole my coat at a soup kitchen while I ate so I took another one—

puffy, polyester filled—and walked on, heading for a "triangle of roads" I remembered

coming out of the woods, having met

those roads but as a young man. Figure

that. The woods came down the hill and stopped and a single

bright road, looping, led up into the recollected triangle—

it was not of course really a triangle but three ways, three lanes into the trees,

that met the bright road in a series of intersections.

I perceived a common drama but saw endless jungle.

                                              Name me, I said.

I had been a handsome woman of indeterminate size and color.

If I were her I'd be a different animal, said I, I'd be

down on the coast, I'd

have made a plan.

Were I she, I'd likely be a monster's dark mother, I thought.

I didn't know when to stop.

The mountain intervened—

unhidden, foul-figured.

Ask me.

(Name it.)

Vividness can be misleading.

I don't know where to stop. Name

another ending.

Third Dream

(for Lyrae Van Clief-Stefanon)

I had come to a transit center, tucked

into a hillside, and the trains were up a long staircase but the buses came in

at street level and in the lowest haunt were stalls where those not

running were parked with doors propped wide open; I was down there

at the foot of the mountain

with them—there was *statuary*, there was

a mild nausea which, dreaming,

I'd mistaken for evil, and

also a jaguar (a big one, stocky

and unexpected) slouching

through, amid the bus bays.

But I was a colored doctor

(in the dream)

in shirtsleeves and a silk tie

and I patrolled the concourses

and the platforms too, where the trains were.

Trains are a distraction, like "explaining" Negro luck

and no skilled stagehand present to act out

what Negro luck might really *be* on the mountain.

I was a rolling avatar in the dream of the station, on

patrol, a country doctor, an image.

Follow the rime of the mustache's turn

and twitch

(*dream that!*)

with its cigarette.

Tuck in.

Suture me.

Count that.

Aloof then, I'd have patrolled such natural boundaries.

So country.

A train was leaving, and I ran alongside for a time—down the platform—before I
    understood

I couldn't keep up so I found my car and "gave chase" that way, following the tracks out

into the toolies because I knew how to do that—because

I have a railroad sense—

and kept to the state roads through "bad" mountain towns

and would catch sight of the train on other hillsides, ones parallel

to the ridges I was driving on—I'd

keep watch.

Similarly, the tracks would parallel the main street of each town I came through and

I'd slow and glance left but the crossing lights and gates were not activated so I
  understood

or *decided* that I'd gotten ahead of the train.

(I'd stayed on the two-lanes and watched my speed and got ahead. So *country!*)

Tuck in, I thought, half-awake, laughing, in cool sheets!

Negro luck, rampant on the mountain!

There was a bridge where I'd thought that the train and I would meet, thought that

I'd flag it down at the Susquehanna River crossing.

Sunset was violent . . .

Evil's the *long* story—

it'll slap you silly in the night season!

(*I was on my way to Negro Mountain.*)

It was dusk—*entre chien et loup!*—when I arrived.

Fourth Dream

Typical crime drama in which I was being transferred

to Ohio—going home—for punishment, for execution. From what

place? An older girl was driving me there and others, boys

and girls, were lounging in the back seat but I was handcuffed, somehow,

to the older girl, who was white and who'd been my friend in real—that is, *waking*—
life.

          I was to be pushed from an airplane and I calculated the possibilities

for the execution itself failing, that is,

for surviving the fall, for my abilities saving me—I could simply ride the thermals,
hawk-like, or

I could swing down, as Tarzan would, on a long vine. And, finally,

this was not another country but my Ohio—my terra-cotta landing strip, home
court—so

I thought that it'd be in the cards that I'd not die, or that

I could just *let it go*, if you know what I mean.

          But as we neared the state line I saw how unrealistic that was
and that

I'd have to separate myself from my old friend, this as the country itself turned
familiar, meaning

I saw that we'd come to the colored suburb, the ranch houses

owned by Black physicians (some on low hills, all "well-made," each one set

back from the road but with a long driveway curving, in each instance, to an attached

garage), and that we'd soon come to the intersection by Doctor Ford's place,

at which point—in the dream—I saw that it would all be wild cards.

The countryside was the same old, same old but my friend, into whose

yard I'd been welcomed, and often, as a boy, was a *test*

and I wondered what the "right" moment would be to separate from her after all

these years and then saw I had no plan, at least in the dream.

Like many Negroes, I am

interested in captivity and in the *ideas* of punishment and public sacrifice.

(If your luck *holds* you can outlive the consequences!)

Like most of us I've wanted to come home. Love

could repeat like scenery does or copy itself. You might luck on out vis-à-vis

the competition. My friend—the older girl—and I had shared

neither bed nor hillside bower.

Love's punishment as well, isn't it? Articulate

it over the landscape. Love's poison, daddy, what did you expect? Who's going to be the Tarzan figure after all and who's the blank slate?

                                    Still asleep but I'd started to

wonder if they *expected* me to permit *them*

to go happily on with the execution, to nudge me on out

some growling airplane's door.

I *imagined*—in the dream—the mosaic of half-acre lots, a few

with concrete patios, the fields just beyond those, and Buicks

seeming to float between the STOP signs all down Liberty Road.

Fifth Dream

Returning—from where?—in a hospital ship,

approaching New York Harbor after months at sea. Confined

below deck but free to watch the crew—kitchen boys and the nurses as well, out

on the bow with their cell phones—through my porthole. We

were coming in slow under

zebra skies and glided right past

the colossal Statue

of Liberty and the reek

of *diesel* was everywhere—a smoky dawn indeed!

　　　　But in the dream my situation was ambiguous—at once I was ill, with

a complicated fever, and, also, "simply" returning

to the hospital, up the Hudson River,

where I had worked long before, where I'd use my old knowledge of the wards to

move around inside—I could pass unnoticed, I understood, this

ability or necessity being the frame of some lesson or subplot

in which I was a double agent.

　　　　In fact,

I was a monster in the dream—apparently

narcissistic though ill-featured and grizzly; and "talented," meaning

predatory. Cherish

your grudges, I thought, *dreaming*. Watch

monsters. Waking,

which is to say *now*, I think I'd probably been

dead and was returning from *that*, it

having been impermanent, death having been some location on a trade route—such,

in the dream's economy, that could be reached by conventional water traffic.

But in the dream it

was just a shallow business—that

is, I'd come back willingly but not jubilantly.

Some's

based in memory (the observed

moment on the bow, e.g.) though

I was always to be the visitor.

And—too—I had helped set

a trap for the monster I was, this

split also a tiresome trope, and predictable.

Predictable as well was that the trap—a wooden shark cage—was obviously
    insubstantial.

But, as the visitor, I approached the cage eagerly because it was to have been baited with

"another of my kind" and I anticipated happily ripping it apart and freeing my comrade.

But, upon arrival at the cage, via a series of corridors that brought me to

an interior room in the hospital, I found it empty.

                            By then, though, I was, simply, a white man—I was, by

then, beyond disappointment but was recognized immediately and

detained in the room (confined once more!) until a nurse came and I overpowered
    her and

bade her keep quiet while I escaped.

            Leaving the hospital I stepped into the street and began to run, knowing

I'd be caught, the town being too small for me to melt in. River-mouth town, low tide
    just

stinking up the estuary as I leapt from bridge to bridge! And

began to compose a story that would free *me*, one

that made reference to my doppelganger—the

Black criminal or servant, the faithful one, also "of colossal proportions" but, even

so, dead of his wounds in the jungle, or perhaps it was only

that he was a comedian, memorialized in the papers, having been carried off by
    fever "like

a pioneer"—and how my white freedom would add value to his memory.

                Who was my host in this foolishness between sea and land? What

horse was I riding, what crocodile was this in the services of? Feeling the story's

sham as I stacked it together.

Sixth Dream
(for Kathy G.)

                                     Saw the gaggle of plates

tacked up, shrines—makeshift—to dead friends, white boys

from everyplace, these on fencing that lined the road to the ferry but I stayed with it

instead of slowing to acknowledge the names, those boys who'd died "sensibly," myself

—dreaming—having been in my own hurry to make the boat to Canada this time, to

the jungled islands, to "real life" and, dreaming, I was—typically—on my bicycle,

but then I was running, with a crowd of people, through basements

and we all came to a ragged shore, subterranean gravel against which water lapped, an

empty place . . .

                          So I ran *furiously* and—this time—quite alone from there back

up the staircases I'd descended with all those others and found

the *real* ferry slip—from which the boat to Canada would leave—on an upper level,
     one

unseen from the big hallways we'd run through—the crowd and I—and

the departure horn was *blaring* and another Negro was there,

cranking down the grill gate, so

I dropped and rolled under the gate and he said, *It's okay,*

and then, as the grill touched pavement,

he said, *You're in.*

                              But I'd come down from the mountainside itself

and had maintained the steady pace all my own

(but that *luck*

having held)

                 as I'd roamed the highways, differing

with women and men I'd met in my transit, even

as we'd share meals or beds.

Such contexts! Yet

I was, myself, "inescapable," I thought—even dreaming—but understood myself, big

as I still was, to be so *unnamed* that nothing—

no bridge or green sward—could be "in memorial"

to me, ever. Death's

just money in a bank. At the slip

I said, *We have to wait for my sister.*

Seventh Dream

Tarzan's family was beautiful in the dream, bright

and rambunctious, a sexual disaster for the jungle. But

wolves came back.

(The dreams recur like days of a hot week.)

There's a time of afternoon

when the buses are frequent but this slacks off

—"in the racial cities"—by early evening

and I was dreaming of riding the Number 1 through town

and jungle both—lucky

to have flagged it down at dusk—and finding

the familiar colored suburb to be everywhere and

bigger by half than memory, finding—in fact—

that everywhere

in camp was now Negro in fact and in outlook.

I saw a cloud of rage over the treetops—several

types of argument were apparently at play. Made

by whom? Who was there,

in whose name?

It was dusk and as I rode I saw how Camptown's just a long sleeve

for how the place was ranging—once covered

with white neighborhoods, it was now a *simple* mountain,

the neighborhoods themselves abandoned (the white people

having vamoosed),

and now—in the dream—crisscrossed with animal paths,

the white people's houses gone to ruin as well, and

wolf dens—evidence of the return noted above—all over, up

and down the ridges, the space they'd occupied.

(The dream was typical, a canopy itself for temper's unrehearsed volume.)

Waking, now, the question would be,

What business do the wolves have

on jungle byways, what do they conform to, or offer?

It's how Number 1's in conversation—more so—with the hillside, its

familiar route being the creep over the ridges,

Number 1 being commonality itself described as the moving point,

the move practically a *walk*, in terms of pace.

Overtake me, love.

The Negro Mountains

Portland Parish/ The Blue Mountains

She said,

Get your bearings.

No shape in my gap,

not now.

If this is allied to "the negro

character," it's far

from original—I'd only get

to where

we came *out* of the mountains and

hit the sea. And view

the old coast too, from

the road, the route described

by its indentations—"One bay

after another"—until the road turned inland

again. Civilization's

tattered

in such. Far

be it from me. One's

close to nothing.

Something,

though, to the coast—

"My affection

hath an unknowne bottome, like the Bay

of Portugall," some-

one else had been made

to say.

The Endless Mountains

The Endless Mountains could

as well be the Werewolf Mountains.

Count some days.

The mountains just

repel the story

with their endlessness.

A dusky fellow could give them enough

to not be bothered

by them

for more.

Come, nighttime,

please. The evening wolf

is the necessary wolf.

From now on, don't bother me about it.

Seven Mountains

She said, *It's*

in God's hands

now.

(Evil's

limitless

and multiple

locations

serve.)

Make a rural cure,

doctor, make

a favorable poultice.

Mountains

itch

all over, all

the way

down. The mountaintops

are bare rock in wave-like patterns, there's often

as not

a fat saddle between

the ridges.

Who do you think you saw?

Second sight, second

thought.

Apostrophe's wide,

uncountable.

Mountain's the default.

In real life, it's a tough neighborhood, doctor—

haunted,

in fact.

Nothing's

enough. Count

off.

The Allegheny Plateau

Travel's enigmatic and we don't have to go to Negro Mountain to see that.

Doom being in the details is all there is to know.

Sometimes music creeps forward and slows down to nothing, like an animal could.

The *trace* is fact but content—the dull feeling—is elsewhere.

Form's noise in the bushes.

No bottom to the songs, which must be their charm. Such

is apparent, even

obvious.

The mountain's a ridge on a plateau.

Voices are that noise getting ahead of itself.

It'd seem that certainty's "grounded" in repetition,

one thing on top of another.

The mountain's available.

"Anglicize" that.

What do you travel to to think about anything?

The *bear* went over

the mountain.

I said this before.

Let's be clear, I said then.

Let's be clear—

love, there's no frame in here, there's

nothing but weather on rock.

Carol me.

Speaker's

the werewolf on Negro Mountain, wouldn't

you say, doctor?

Carol me that.

What do you think they saw?

Mt. Davis

Don't mistake the speaker, best

beloved, for the Green Man.

Multiple addresses do abound. So

also don't allow the mountain breeze to fool you, child.

There exist,

hereabouts,

a thousand ways to pass as a gentleman—even

to all you meet—that are smooth

and clear and

untroubled as skin

itself.

But, to *cough*,

from *here* on,

that

would be what

interrupts the air—

the loose coughing

clears the theatre.

A line of crows,

say,

ragtag,

say,

baying.

(Mountain's just got a little doghouse sitting up on its top.)

Thought's nothing but that catch in the throat.

Shaggy Papa,

Papa Bois,

the dusky fellow at roadside.

(What do you do, sir, after such exhaustion, after the cloth's touched flesh, as

it were, after

it's out of you in all this range and space, the

scandalous present?)

Made a mistake?

Certainty's

all out of you, sir,

hesitation articulates the roosts.

Make another, sir.

Crows do skirt the mountain, best beloved.

Event Place/ Beat 5 Camden, Madison, Mississippi, United States.

(1900 Census; Willy Smith, B [for Black], at 5)

Time of day would be the factor but some days wolves could have come,

and easily, along the creeks and rivers and through the cane as well

and the cypress swamps.

(Safe to say, doctor.)

They would have been red wolves, those wolves

—*Canis rufus*, doc—

almost bright-colored (in their descriptions), and *Mississippi*

Negroes, because of working outside then, would have (likely) crossed paths

with such wolves, at work or (possibly

or even more likely) while hunting

(another fair speculation, eh?—and the meat getting ever closer to the bone, persona

yourself, my faithful MD, occupational tattering aside, color intended,

commerce in souls and spirit to be avoided but you still being the gentle priest—
    ancestry-

dot-com, good brother—and no endless plateau, low land in its place coming

to mind as *pure* speculation, formless,

but do no harm, Mister Obeah, foist nothing)

and the *swamps*, here—in this location—also repel the story, and

terms besiege us.

(Got that one right, root-man!

Not a mountain in sight—umber, curse-color, or crowed—to offer opinions about
   any

kind of wolf thereupon.)

Disfigure me, think it over, bring a shape like it was medicine.

Interested speakers came through the scene.

(Old Natchez Trace being just over there.)

We didn't *have* to go to Negro Mountain.

Crow, baby!

Question comes up again like bioluminescence: the educated speaker

might ask, What's the alliance between red wolves and the Negro character?

Pine forests.

Comment l'insolent!

(Impatiently.) Have you guessed it or not?

From just *what* is the voice speaking?

Absence in the swamp, brother.

Negroes in the wildwood!

Close as we're gonna get.

No moon.

Extirpated now, am I right, doc?

Bald Eagle Mountain

I'm as interested in Bellefonte as I am

                            on the mountain: there's

the mild nausea, there's having had "a presentiment,"

there not being, apparently, enough white to the world.

                                      Measure it against

the downturned mouth of Negroid displeasure.

                    Trace the hill, readers, study the Negro frontier, rest

in the shadow, let such fall

                         and fall and fall and clang.

(Or make note of the addresses herein, let

                vexed be also a kind of interest, a two-hander

        for certain.)

                One wishes, doctor, for an educated listener.

Just look over their heads, she would say.

Camptown

1.
Camptown's the long foot of Negro Mountain.

Please yourself, form's harsh and anything

could slip across a bridge in the wee

hours, when traffic's not heavy, from one place

or another to Camptown.

Please yourself.

I was a ship on the stormy ocean—stay off me, brother,

I write from bottomless description and

I still might be a monster.

2.
Camptown's no argument. Dogs

know what dogs want.

But a *gentleman's* definite in his address, his

gait's confident (and the walk overlaps

with the *pace* of a likely monster).

Fleur dans sa boutonnière, 'tit Banjo . . .

A gentleman's the apex of style,

Mais laid jus' comme le Diab'!

The devil's in the bushes, brother man.

Camptown's just *splayed* between the mountain and the wolves.

All the parts are speaking parts.

3.
In town the boys were jumping.

Say that the door survives the fiery house,

or say the story's navigable

all day, all

the way up

to a point and

all the way down. Voices

strain the escarpment

and tunes come down off

the slope to image monstrosity.

Sing the thing, Brother Schism!

Sing the affection.

Measure that, daddy!

Camptown's wind in the window, wind

come right down through backyards to snag your attention.

Expect *me*.

The devil's in the long, long song.

Camptown?

In God's hands now.

4.
Study what's left of requiescats.

We raced all day—

and a day is full of parts—and then

nighttime came

and here came doom down the street to please you and

oh how comfortable the monstrous peaks

—like in song, baby—

and how navigable!

Voice can get you to it, voice

is *wolfish*, sugar,

it's just old charisma.

5.
There's some evil to this conveyance.

Flesh and fable both.

In one passage I was *colossal.*

(Monstrous stays evil all *day.*)

Dusk just paces itself,

under the laurel.

So unstated,

so cat-eyed.

In another I was *reliable.*

Brother, who—in hell—walks?

There's a dusky fellow in the populace

—a well-read splib for every deliberation—

and just as outside as outside can be as well.

6.
Keep your distance.

I may not be the monster you'd take me for.

The dreams—in which Camptown appears—recur like those *segmented* buses.

(The mountain allows me my separate angers.)

Trace the trolley wires and note the unmarked loops.

Do me like a phrase, curse

me on the pavement like I was a dog!

A low *haunt's* bottomless.

(I'd tarry in the dooryard and then I would take my leave.)

7.
Please yourself.

In Camptown the lit-up buses dance like "sea-shapes" out

among all the lights as though Camptown was, in fact, the whale road.

We shall see what we shall see.

(Keep your distance.)

One *waits* on the bus—walk over, dark coming in all the ways dark

comes, or right here already—as

though colossal time was complicated or intimate or

overlapped with you.

Overlapping Apexes
(for Ed Roberson)

1. The Negro Mountains

In 1802 Lady Nugent wrote, on the occasion of her visit to St. Thomas in the East (near Kingston, Jamaica, B.W.I.)—

My usual levee of coloured ladies. One told me she was twenty-four years old, and shewed me her grand-child. I found afterwards that she was fifty-four; but they have no idea of time or distance. They reckon the one by the number of Christmas masquerades they can recollect, and for the other they have no scale. If you ask how far to such a place, they will say, "two or tree mile," if it should be twelve or fourteen. If it exceeds that, they say, "far enough, massa," or "too far, massa."

And, later that year, on her visit to the Maroons of Charles Town, at the bottom of the Blue Mountains in Portland Parish, Lady Nugent wrote—

The Maroons received us as if they were much pleased with our visit; the women danced, and the men went through their war exercise for us. The dancing was exactly like that of the negroes at Christmas, and their military manuvres seemed to consist entirely of ambuscade; taking aim at their enemy from behind trees, leaping up, and rolling about, to avoid being wounded themselves.

Altogether it was so savage and frightful, that I could not help feeling a little panic, by merely looking at them.

Out of reach of what's come for me I write from *measureless* location. Often

enough, shouts come over an embankment—instructions,

deft ironies, the causal—but, in fact, relief's really only relief from what

"barking" there is inside so *do* please yourself, I'm thinking, and don't *get* cross with me.

Our faithlessness, our specific ability to navigate on and off the mountain, is divided

in fact. That is, unchanging, I am really any animal. That is, I

identify with them who have hunting enemies and "acknowledge" the enemies that would flay them as well.

I write—or did or have written—from "Victorian" Bellefonte (over Bald Eagle
  Mountain

from the Allegheny Front's *different* forest)

and from Tangletown, near Bellefonte.

I write this morning from California.

And were you really to ask, I'd reply that there's

nothing ahead but more of the similar, the same old slope—that is, there's no snag song,

the devil's in the *water* (and so hot the common element!), and it's no matter

to me what names you address me as.

2. *Panthera onca*

How in the world do you know?

Reading.

Explanatory, justificatory.

The fur rubbed away beneath the collar.

You come again and over again to the mercenary.

Apprehension, someone said, or the double, exact down to the number of teeth, to
"the surface of the brain."

Fine Mister Stedman, his *Narrative, of a five years' expedition; against the revolted negroes of Surinam: in Guiana, on the wild coast of South America; from the year 1772, to 1777.*

Or, on the other hand, Mister Roberson, from a 2010 interview—

We had set up camp not realizing we were this close to the volcano. When we were making camp, the air had cleared and we had seen it for the first time. That night we had built lean-tos and had fires. We woke up during the night and the Indians were carrying on, and the one who spoke a little bit of Spanish said that a jaguar had passed by to get something to drink. Thank goodness he wasn't hungry, only thirsty! But there were tracks. The idea was that we were sharing the night together. The jaguar had passed through camp. So the image is that the jaguar is there, but you don't see him.

Like all of us in the family. The persistent cough, throat clearing.

From the beginning.

"Tyger, tyger." First poem.

The Maroons crossed the Marowijne River into *French* Guiana and then the campaign was over, it having succeeded in making Surinam "uncomfortable," at least for a while.

Love gets beyond itself even in diffusion. In fluidity.

Look at me.

A Negro man at work in his garden; or on the stage—an actor—or in the club car, the Lead Service Attendant. Reading the *New Yorker*. Late, under lamplight, in his office on Home Avenue. In the alley. On a street in Bronzeville. At the bottom of the stairs, reciting for his child.

What did I know? Ask it twice.

There's a disconnect between being "fluid" and being "revealed"—captured at the time of transition, "caught," as it were—at the transgressive or transgressing moment. Quitting the territory. "By canoe in two groups," went the description of the exit. 1776, 1777.

Merry gentlemen.

O.E.D. said, "jaguara or jagua is originally a class-name for all carnivorous beasts, including the tiger (i.e., jaguar), the puma, etc., more recently also extended to dogs, the specific name of the jaguar being jaguareté, where -eté is a Tupi augmentative, generally rendered 'true.'"

Where does a gentleman stop? Keep your distance, sir.

O.E.D. said, in the examples of usage, that in 1796 John Gabriel Stedman, in his account of the "seemingly endless series of maroon uprisings," wrote, "It has even happened that the jaguar has carried off young negro women at work in the field."

Peel head John Crow sit up on the treetop.

JUTA bus goes by, windows agape.

Apparent and eccentric blackness, the *root* of design.

(Dusky fellow at the wheel.)

Return of the Charles-Town Maroons, 1st November 1831:
Among those represented, Fanny Giscome, second oldest—at 80—on the roster of "Invalids and Superannuated" Maroons. (Her slaves too—James Shackleford, Benjamin Cameron, Louisa Cameron, and Edward.)

"The dogs were a wild-looking set," said the President on a jaguar hunt, he having thought that they had red wolf in them.

The fox just *endures* the trap, she or he endures being the trap and being the fox, both.

For me, gents, it's cats *and* dogs.

Entre perro y lobo.

Revelation comes in stages to the one on trail, no parable there, sir—twilight's just the base for darkness.

Pure meaning "perfect." Discriminatory prowess. What's it like?

Now, some evenings it's just too cold to work in the fields.

Speakerly colored boy with a downturned mouth—autumn in his face like one thing and another—and "taken" with wild birds, having read *Life in Many Lands,* having fallen in as well with carnivora—"big" cats, the wild dogs—even if from a distance.

Call God's name. Say you're his friend.

Borges said, "I imagined my god confiding his message to the living skin of the jaguars, who would love and reproduce without end, in caverns, in cane fields, on islands, in order that the last men might receive it. I imagined that net of tigers, that teeming labyrinth of tigers, inflicting horror upon pastures and flocks in order to perpetuate a design." (This was in a story.)

(The devil's on the mountain, jaguars in the yard.)

I never came *back* from anywhere, your speaker writes.

Strange cats began to drift over the border, wander into sight.

(*I myself come from over the mountain.*)

What I *knew* about shape—water from a faucet, water in a bowl. Jouncy hindquarters down the hill. Shape? Don't. Don't say a single thing.

Love's instinct, though; love devours you. Love's got no animal, even if it's supposed to have one or some. Some of them or one animal, which would speak or loom, either one, for all of them.

Ed Roberson has opined on the nature of my "West Indian stutter."

The idea that "the shaman was a jaguar or at least a spotted predator."

Twenty-eight years previously Fanny Giscome—at fifty-three—probably knew Lady Nugent was going to be coming to Charles Town.

Time's *come* today. Wrath, etc., is everywhere, today.

Pure evil. All day.

So go on and shift the shape—divinity, interruption itself. To waiting, no wisdom coming or offered.

To wait on someone who wears meaning you can see or almost see. A gentleman wears a jacket because the jacket rule applies. Do you wish to be served? "An ordinary Negro gentleman" in a jacket.

The shoulder of South America just hunches along the Atlantic. Demerara, sugar.

Charles Town's a mile in from Buff Bay.

We—your speaker's people—were also from *around* the "great house" above the bay.

(Listen for the addresses.)

Homeborn slaves, the family was "native." It's a short walk over the mountains.

The light-skinned novelist said, "There's always a West Indian involved in the fracas somewhere." In conversation, in Islands talk, Stedman comes up as often as not.

"Ruckus gonna come."

In St. Elizabeth—down by Treasure Beach—people say the crocodiles bark to lure dogs to their doom.

(Broadgate, Stony Hill, rich Constant Spring.)

Sangay Volcano's seventy-seven hours, by car, from Paramaribo or Par'bo, formerly Fort Willoughby.

Sometimes it's too hot to sleep.

Some danger, some beauty. Scorn the lyrics. Haunt the road, overlap.

Apex predator at the door, at the northern window, popped suddenly out of its pajamas.

As it were. Shape don't cut no ice.

Expect jaguars. Watch crocodiles. Consider wolves.

Ed said that he "could see sentences within sentences."

Dogs and crocodiles were thought to share a language.

Terms trail the animal, they're a nuisance.

The words come to me, two-thirds asleep, like a warning—*not a literal jaguar*. Spoken.

Comparison, specificity, verbs.

(I write today from ample California. This had been Mexico.)

We—the fox-king of the hills, old and sandy-colored, and your speaker—met on the road, once, when he crossed in front of the bicycle and waited.

William Blake had made some of the engravings for *Revolted Negroes* and later became friends with Stedman, whose descriptions could have "fed" the poem— mentioned above—in "Songs of Experience," this in speculation.

Tenzing Norgay was the Tiger of the Snows.

Communicate with me a little bit. What're you asking of me? What do you want me to see? What do you want *me* to look at? What if I don't?

Hawk Mountain's in Pennsylvania and the website says how the red-tails—Buteo jamaicensis—often, or often enough, "hunt along Interstate Highways, and are sometimes called roadside hawks."

Work's work. You show up, do the job, and—*if your luck holds*—you go home.

"Shiny eye," "a thousand things."

The wolves come to me, unspeaking, like nothing else.

Tigers?

We came west on the California Zephyr. We boarded easily, we'd set out in the morning.

Rousseau's famous painting is called, sometimes, *The Virgin Forest*. Also, *Jungle with Setting Sun*. Too, *Jaguar Attacking a Negro*. (*Nègre attaqué par un jaguar* dit aussi *Paysage de forêt vierge au soleil couchant*.) "The primitive can be seen as the inhabitant of an earthly paradise."

The print's widely available, it's wallpaper.

We came through undefined country, west of Denver. Parts of Colorado had been parts of Mexico.

The jaguar, the "ruddy" bandito, and the poem aren't one.

Hold on to your money, keep your distance.

L.S.A. in a blue vest working, at a table in the dining car, on the Builder, the Starlight, the Zephyr.

Shade, leaf-shadow, scat cat!

Here the old animal goes, *trailing shape*, some splib said.

And he said, I really *am* any animal.

Nothing causal.

Unbounded recitative; a "wandering Negress, a mandolin player."

"The were-jaguar of the Olmecs . . . is a compound image with non-jaguar parts drawn from other life forms."

Similarly, the wolves, the Negro "speaker," and the mountain are not one.

Panthera onca came through Penn's Woods. Pleistocene range was at least as far as Bone Cave, Montgomery County, four hours, or so (by car), due east of Negro Mountain.

Jaguar sky, somebody said.

A jaguar's the king of *all* the ghosts.

I write from the backyards.

Use one dog to catch the other ones. (Must I repeat myself?)

Jaguar's like a definition in a thicker scenery.

(Dogs know.)

Music appears (again!) and what do you see in it, dear?

Burn bright, baby! Recite, recite!

(What do you *say*?)

Ed Roberson said—

As if we are always asleep

the end comes
right up to us and stares into our sleeping eyes,
ignores us and continues on its way.

Far enough.

Enough! or Too much!

(Don't be long.)

Notes on Region

Wolves came back to Negro Mountain. There was no pattern to it, for either mountain or animals to occupy—it was not a story but rather the germ of a shape, an undetectable weight; it was shapeless finally, unmeasured, it was only relayed.

Negro Mountain—the summit of which, as noted above, is the highest point in Pennsylvania—is a default, a way (among others) to think about the Commonwealth.

Meshach Browning wrote, "The Negro Mountain is so called because, after Braddock's defeat on the Monongahela, a scouting party, traveling Braddock's Road, came in contact with a like party of Indians, when a skirmish ensued, in which one Indian was killed, and a very large negro mortally wounded."

Perhaps the variation of wolves and other dogs is a series of false dilemmas. Any speaker might stand—or be "placed" and decry—in their midst. In fact, the *territories* overlap; the territories are the same series—*plural*—of fields, trees, elevations, and watercourses. A coyote—called prairie wolf also, or "barking dog," or *medicine wolf*, or brush wolf—is a wolf. (Foxes are a different matter.) *Canis lycaon*—the Great Lakes wolf—was named for the king Zeus turned into a wolf. Neighborhood dogs bark in a chain, children know this.

"The red wolf of the south is smaller," noted Zim and Hoffmeister.

Word came from Negro Mountain that a lifelong resident there had surprised a wolf in her dooryard. Summer 2016. Her carpenter, she said, had also seen the wolf, on a separate occasion. Not a coyote—the population that has flourished in Pennsylvania since the 1930s—but a wolf.

One is similar to another.

Henry Shoemaker said, "The only person killed was the colonel's favorite Negro body servant, a black of colossal proportions. The Indians were driven off, and the body of the unfortunate Negro dropped down in a deep crevice of the rocks in a shoulder of the mountain, and the party resumed its way."

(Talk on top of one another, you mountains.)

Entre chien et loup.

What Negro?

(Lie atop one another, anybody could say.)

Pennsylvania man, half jungle animal, talking.

It varies.

On such a mountain a deliberate Negro man, or a pensive Negro man, might wish to be "spirited away." Industry is a deep valley or a trough. Zora Neale Hurston wrote, "Mules and other brutes had occupied their skins." There is a long bottom to consider—not the path of a moving figure, but the swath. "Opposite" deep valleys are the hills, elevations; a common enough wish is to enter such places and/or climb through them. Often enough one sees death in the market, or at work in an office, "under fluorescent light," explaining; someone else might see death come across the summit, like weather. Death is worked toward, death is "explained." Such a Negro man might wonder what he needed to know, for the sake of coherence, and find the qualification daunting, or amusing.

    Among you.
          It could be the figures' motion. Between the reader
and, say, the poem or the mountain at hand.
                      Speaker, observer,
                              Negro, poet, wolf, measure. *All you.*

Thomas Cresap (of the Ohio Company, a land speculator, a captain in the Maryland Militia, "usually called 'the English Colonel'") had, by 1749 or 1750, established a friendship with the hereditary Delaware chief Nemacolin and had helped him—Nemacolin—"lay out" a trail from the Potomac River to the Monongahela River. John Bedell, for the National Parks Service, wrote, "Over the years the trail would come to be known by several names, including Nemacolin's Trail and Braddock's Road."

Mrs. Stevenson's 1901 account: "June 30th, 1756, Col. Cresap and his party had another skirmish with the savages. He had not forgotten the lamented sleeper [Thomas Cresap, Jr., killed in the earlier 'skirmish'] on Savage Mountain; he enlisted another company of volunteers, taking with him his two surviving sons Daniel and Michael and a gigantic negro servant, belonging to him. . . . This time they advanced into the wilderness as far as a mountain, a mile west of Grantsville. There, they met the Indians; a fight took place and the negro Goliath was slain, and the mountain has been 'Negro Mountain' ever since."

Spirit is no sum; nor is it a *factor* of determination. Or, better, *content*.

In Rumsey's online collection, Negro Mountain begins appearing on Pennsylvania maps with John Melish's "Map of Pennsylvania," published in 1822. It appears on Henry Tanner's 1823 "Pennsylvania and New Jersey" and on the 1849 Barnes map as well.

What else might a Negro *speaker* ask?

The eastern forest is no theater. There is a very long shadow in the forest. The forest harbors "game" and predators. There's a curious blankness that, *like* song or theater, is comforting but that sits outside the fact of silence; there's an angry sky, often, over valley towns—Somerset, say, or Bellefonte, the tiny county seat at the base of Bald Eagle Mountain—that extends to the clouds above the mountain. One day there is a hawk screaming on a tree branch and another one, silent, itself above a field, in the near distance, both visible from a road over the mountain. Perhaps a third hawk is nearby, unseen by the observer. Another day one arrives—say at midafternoon, at a *place* where some lanes converge into a series of triangle shapes at the base of a Pennsylvania mountain or a *location* on the mountain's flank—and finds the intersections empty.

(There's bottomless *absence*; there is obvious failure. And grief. You know how unstable they are.)

The idea is that wolves are—in the twenty-first century Commonwealth—"unlikely." Perhaps, at best, it is that there's an opacity to a Pennsylvania forest that such an animal—a wolf, say, in the present context or location of subject and trajectory and rumor—is *similar* to. Such an animal would be familiar—that is, recognizable in terms of shape and size and perhaps most profoundly in its movements—were it to appear, an act for which the observer might wish. In the Ridge and Valley region of the state the roads are often empty. A Negro speaker might ask what he—or she— was expected to represent in the field or at roadside or between the trees. Intimacy might be an answer; bottomless *intimacy*—in terms of the familiar *knowledge* or claim of such or recognition of it in among the trees—is "naturally" ungainly. Or coarse.

Negro Mountain's a ridge on the same long plateau as the Endless Mountains; however, its appearance is that of "low relief." Shape fails; finally, perhaps, it's how you—meaning the speaker and the reader as well—*perceive* the shape failing since all that's too large to accommodate by sight or by any of the senses. Of the Llano Estacado—
of West Texas, called "the Staked Plains" by Kenneth Irby and others and described by Irby as a region the loneliness of which is "like the love of death"—a correspondent from Denver writes, "The slope is imperceptible to an observer on the plateau"; representation, a kind of dexterity or sleight of hand—once again—places one. The shape *shifting*, however, is irreducible, is interruption itself.

(Argument'll take shape. Long after the argument—in an open place, say, or in a passage between houses—comes something wild.)

The Endless Mountains of northeast Pennsylvania, "a great series of parallel, heavily forested ranges," are a geographic barrier and they—the Endless Mountains themselves—are a dissected plateau, eroded, having been "formed after regional uplift."

(Now—2018—they're fracking there.)

A movie Negro would detach himself from the shade at the roadside of the Endless Mountains, looking "distinguished" and, being a speaker, in possession of "regular features." Let's see. There was a big fellow in the forest. *Fetch him.* If you *cross* the Endless Mountains you'll come to Negro Mountain but when you're in them you are only following the skyline. Let's see.

Generations of Pennsylvania wolves had "denned up" on a boulder-strewn shoulder on the north side of Negro Mountain, a location still—in 2018—called the Wolf Rocks.

Hawk Mountain, in the Ridge and Valley region, is a funded sanctuary for predatory birds of passage and for vultures—which are not predatory—as well. Updrafts and thermals peculiar to the location carry such birds over the mountain—that is, the traveling broad-winged raptors (eagles, turkey vultures and black vultures, buteos such as red-tailed hawks, etc.) and the accipiters (sharp-shinned hawks, Cooper's hawks, and the like) make use of the trick of air currents in their migrations, ascending in spiral currents of warm air—thermals—and then, having gained altitude, following the ridges subsequent to Hawk Mountain. Hawk Mountain is itself yet another ridge, as is Negro Mountain. (The description of Negro Mountain's prominence mentioned above is from the Hyperleap website: "The mountain is flattish in appearance due to its location on the Allegheny Plateau, so its prominence is of low relief.") The mountains—Hawk and Negro—are 250 miles distant from one another. Between them—the deep forest of the Seven Mountains and, of course, the curve of the Appalachians.

Perhaps the big Negro at hand was, in effect, a country doctor. Versed, practical, aloof.

The mountain intervenes. The mountains intervene.

Performance at a scattershot mill town at the bottom of the hills. The skinny Negro at the door to the theater said, *Take your dinner in*. He said, *Don't lose your money*. He said, *Remember where you put it*—the money—at the mouth of the theatre. *Remember what you did with it*, he said.

On one hand is the lively narration in *Peter and the Wolf*—one hears oboe, flute, clarinet, and an orchestra's string section and is told that these represent animals and children. The wolf, however, is three French horns. (Or on one book cover the wolf's a Harlequin, all red-vested, upright, and loose-limbed in boots and top hat, juggling a garland of post horns.)

The set piece "First Dream" (above) places wolves in the yard of a house itself situated at the Negro edge of a small city and establishes that they were moving in a wave across grass and driveway. The transcription would suggest that the dreamt-of wolves had only come out to where they could be *seen*.

In 2011, vonHoldt et al. worked toward mapping the natural history of "charismatic wolf-like canids"; the focus of their interest had been to "assess long-standing questions about diversification and admixture" of such animals and they noted that the species at hand, "the gray wolf (*Canis lupus*), red wolf (*C. rufus*), Great Lakes wolf (*C. lycaon* or *C. lupus lycaon*), and coyote (*C. latrans*) . . . are characterized by high mobility and weak patterns of intraspecific differentiation [and that,] similarly, large dispersal distances have led to the formation of extensive admixture zones in North America, where four morphologically distinguishable wolf-like canids"—those named just above—"can potentially interbreed." Their focus, in part, had to do with eastern animals and they were criticized by Rutledge et al.—in 2012 in *Biological Conservation*—for their study's "ascertainment bias" and because of "the presence of two wolf types in eastern North America [being] recorded in historical accounts," these in 1859, 1842, and 1672. Of interest here, because of the reported Negro Mountain sightings, is that the vonHoldt group's "latter two taxa"—the Great Lakes wolf and the coyote—"are of controversial ancestry and species status and readily hybridize with other wolf-like canids."

An animal's what people think they see in the jungle.

Leaning on earlier work by Lynda Rutledge and others, Thiel and Wydeven, for the Fish and Wildlife Service (2011), had already iterated that "Algonquin Provincial Park in east-central Ontario is considered by most geneticists to be the geographic core of current *Canis lycaon* distribution in eastern North America (Sears et al. 2003; Grewal et al. 2004; Rutledge et al. 2010a)" and that "immediately south of Algonquin Provincial Park [and] extending across the lower Great Lakes and south of the St. Lawrence Seaway lies the *suture zone* between eastern wolves and coyotes (Kolenosky and Standfield 1975; Sears et al. 2003; Grewal et al. 2004; Kays et al. 2009; Way et al. 2010; Rutledge et al. 2010a). Within this zone eastern wolves admix[ed] with coyotes that began a west-to-east invasion of the region sometime following 1900 (Nowak 2002; Kays et al. 2008, 2009; Wilson et al. 2009; Wheeldon et al. 2010b). . . . South of Algonquin Provincial Park, in an area referred to as the Frontenac Axis, the major genetic ancestry consists primarily of coyote admixed with eastern wolf (Wilson et al. 2009). This trend is observed east into New England and *further south in western Pennsylvania*, New York and Massachusetts (Kays et al. 2009; Way et al. 2010)." Italics added.

The Frontenac Axis is the southern extension of the Canadian Shield. Algonquin Park—where the Halfkenny brothers, George and Mark, and their white friend Billy Rhindress, teenagers all, met death in a bear encounter—is to its north. The boys had been fishing at Radiant Lake. "Those investigating the incident felt that the first boy who was killed, George Halfkenny, may have been attacked because he resembled another bear. George wore dark clothing and was black." This in 1978.

A "thread" on a white supremacist message board bemoaned the presence of Negroes on the Hawk Mountain website. One writer, "treblemaker," who claimed to have recently discovered Hawk Mountain, expressed the fear that Negroes would "begin showing up at this last (nigger free) sanctuary." This in 2009.

The 2011 Fish and Wildlife Service piece presses *suture zones* throughout. "Good evidence exists for the long-term presence of contact or suture zones that extend along the periphery of eastern wolf range. Presently eastern wolves are sympatric with gray wolves to the north; sympatric with gray wolves and coyotes to the northwest (Western Great Lakes region); and to the southeast they are sympatric to (northeastern) coyotes, and in former times, red wolves."

Mix, and match it, match the mix; the thinking overlaps and goes and goes and goes without saying.

In the twentieth century wolves or something similar *crossed into the States—into the northeast and/or the Great Lakes states including of course Pennsylvania—and/or across other borders via railroad bridges (from Canada in the dead of blackest fucking night), a feat of migration or a surmise concerning migration recently mentioned "somewhere" as a likely fact which your speaker, as a child in the years* following *the aforementioned dream of wolves in the yard, had conjectured and then assumed to be a possibility or, as he would recall it—the early conjecture—in 2018, necessity itself.*

A little quiet goes a long way. All dogs range and are, in practice, scavengers. All—a trait—are communal. Dogs know.

Cristina Eisenberg wrote, "During the mid-Pleistocene epoch, about 700,000 years ago, successive waves of wolves returned to North America from Eurasia." Then she wrote, having skipped backwards, "The wolf genus, *Canis* developed in North

America in the late Miocene epoch, about 10 million years ago. . . . By the early Pleistocene epoch, 1.5 million years ago, wolves had split off from coyotes and crossed into Eurasia via the Bering Land Bridge, where they continued to evolve into *C. lupus*, which means 'dog wolf.'" The idea being that they went to Siberia and then came back "different."

How unlikely, then, would it be for a wolf to have appeared—to have shown itself—on Negro Mountain? What might the field marks have been? Summers, writing on observable phenomena, said, "sometimes it is a fantastical shape." But what is a wolf?

Negro what?

The observation or claim that *paradise is full of tremendous images* is something a Negro might make or might have said; that Paradise is incomplete without both the appearance and the sharp absence of its predators is a different animal. One animal's a color—such is description—and the other's God. What's your real name? a young man or woman might ask. I'm the only dog on the plateau, somebody might respond. Measure is measure, any given day. I can teach you image (said an old gentleman), but you won't like it.

The homes of white families populate the slopes of Negro Mountain—it stretches behind their houses as though it were an unspoken-of Negro wife. Somerset County, Wikipedia says, is "1.59% Black or African American" and Negro Mountain straddles the Mason-Dixon Line. Florence Mars wrote, "My other grandfather . . . told me that after the civil war it was customary for former slaveholders to build a house in the back yard and retain one of the better-looking Negro women."

Spoken Commonwealth history of Negro Mountain has preserved the particular Negro's name as having been Nemises, often that spelling, though it would seem unlikely that his parents called him that, it being more likely that he was, in some way, *owned*. Nemises or Nemesis is a mascot's name, a pet's name, the ironic name of an animal. A "name" for *the primitive*. But *Oxford English Dictionary*: Nemesis was "the goddess of retribution or vengeance, who reverses excessive good fortune, checks presumption, and punishes wrongdoing"—continuing, widening—"(hence) a person who or thing which avenges, punishes, or brings about someone's downfall; an agent of retribution," the name having lost, over time, its feminine cast or association.

Consider opposite that the namelessness of the fact of Grendel's mother. And/or consider the loa Marinette Bras Cheche or Marinette Pied Cheche, like Nemesis associated with punishment and retribution and often, one reads, in the company of werewolves, "who hold services in her honor" (Corbett and Chatland, n.d.). "*Nombre de sorciers, porteurs du 'point loup garou,' ont la capacité de se changer durant la nuit en animal. . . . La proximité de ces [âmes perdues] avec des mauvais esprits rôdant dans les campagnes, épousant parfois l'allure de monstres, évoque les noms de Ti-Jean Pied Chèche, Ezili-jé-rouge, Marinette-bois-chèche . . .*" (Elysee 2018).

Or that Margaret Atwood dreamt she was watching an opera she'd written about Susanna Moodie. She wrote, as description of the dream: "I was alone in the theatre: on the empty white stage, a single figure was singing." And she wrote that Susanna Moodie imagined her husband to be a loup-garou but that she—Susanna Moodie—would have him change *her*, "with the fox eye, the owl / eye, the eight-fold / eye of the spider"—every example a predator—and that she would be *unable* to "think / what he will see / when he opens the door."

A question had come up for discussion at the foot of the Blue Mountains in Portland Parish, Jamaica, B.W.I., the same season, summer 2016. The question, open to debate: Can a loa appear to a white person?

What *did* the Negro Mountain woman see when she opened her door on Negro Mountain?

Colonel Thomas Cresap's letter—or an "extract" of the letter—was published in the *Pennsylvania Gazette* on June 6, 1756. (The date contradicts Mrs. Stevenson's account above.) Colonel Cresap wrote, "I made no Halt as the Indians came towards me, but marched up with my Gun cocked on my shoulder. As soon as the Indians came clear of a Bent that was in the Road, about 30 Yards from me, an old Negroe presented his Gun at them; upon which they immediately alighted from their Horses. I saw two run to one Side of the Road, and one to the other, and take Trees. We having no Advantage of Trees at that Place, two of the Indians fired, and shot the Negroe [. . .]."

Or a wolf's figure is the figure that one might tease out of any thought about the woods and hillsides.

The wolf is the thought.

The wolf's the bigger trace of Negro luck.

One might have the wolf say, *I'll measure you.*

Or the wolf might say, *Wish for everything.* The best thing's the thing that's most available.

(Or at the very, *very* best one might be the hawk and the road, both.)

The shift itself—to the listener or reader or observer—may be "imperceptible." It can't be traded; measure falls off.

For what is labor exchanged on the mountain?

It—the *trade* itself—might be theater. Or *like* theater; or song. Sing for your supper, goes one imperative; hold on to your money, confides the second one. The Cresap Society's bulletin from the 1919 meeting at Cumberland: "Colonel Thomas owned a negro of giant stature called Nemesis. In mustering his company the Colonel said 'Nemesis, wont you go with us this time, you are a good shot, and help us conquer these Indians who are murdering and scalping women and children and burning their cabins.' Nemesis considered for a few minutes and then said 'Yes, Massa. I go, but I wont come back.' 'Why, Nemesis, why say that,—you are a sure shot and fearless.' 'Massa Tommie sure shot and afraid of nothing and he not come back. I say I go but I not come back.' His premonition, second sight, was correct. Among the first to fall was the brave slave, and now and forever the mountain where he died is called Negro Mountain."

Colonel Cresap's letter to the *Gazette* had continued, attesting to the unhappy fates of his son, Thomas (the "lamented sleeper" in Mrs. Stevenson's account, "Massa Tommie" mentioned just above), and a Native, who had also perished. "We saw no Bones, but great Signs of Wolves, Turkey Buzzards and Ravens having been at the Place, and make no Doubt of his dying there; for the Bears and Wolves had eaten up another Indian that was scalped at the same time that he was shot, and had scratched up the Body of Thomas Cresap, and eaten it likewise."

In 2018 Nemacolin Woodlands Resort—or, simply, Nemacolin—is a luxury hotel situated on the National Road (U.S. 40), thirty miles west of Negro Mountain.

We don't *have* to go to Negro Mountain but encountering its *sign* on one of the Commonwealth's byways calls for the traveler's attention to the public—meaning widely promoted—roles assigned to African-descended people in North America's popular histories of conquest, annihilation, and supremacy. "The negro Goliath," referenced above, was made to present himself on the stage and speak his tribute to the hall and then die.

Wolves came back.

Second day of bear season in the Commonwealth—November 20, 2017—and my friend met my train at Cumberland and drove me to Negro Mountain to visit the white woman who had seen the wolf, mentioned above. I was the stranger on Negro Mountain, which we crossed that day, in her—my friend's—car, in a trip that included passing the Wolf Rocks and pausing to hike the short distance to the Baughman Rocks, where we pho-tographed one another in the snow. And later drove to Jumonville to climb the knob to the base of the Great Cross of Christ. I was indeed a tremendous stranger on Negro Mountain but I had lived in Bellefonte, Pennsylvania—and had had a railroad life there and had taught writing and image, for some years, at the state university nearby—and had joined or been pulled into conversations specific to the location, though I was neither "English" nor "Dutch" and was not a Philadelphia Negro either. But my friend—herself a white Pennsylvania woman—had not thought to inform the Negro Mountain woman (also white, as noted) that she would, in fact, be bringing a Negro to visit and the woman— who was ninety or more and had taught in the public schools on and near Negro Mountain and had been born in the house in which we visited her—ignored me and spoke only to my friend and was irritated, seemingly, by the question she—the friend—posed having to do with the mountain's name. It was Civil War time, she replied, and an army regiment came through. "They had a Negro with them," she said, and then said that the Negro ran to get away and they chased him and killed him and buried him on the mountain. And the wolf? I asked, finally, interrupting, Did you see a wolf outside? "That was a long time ago," she said, "it's a little fuzzy."

Charismatic Pennsylvania man, upending Leopold, could himself ask, What might the charismatic wolf-like canids sense on the Negro Mountain?

What had the Negro Mountain woman seen, sitting at the kitchen table across from her on Negro Mountain itself?

I had seen a wolf skin in St. Ignace, on the Mackinac Straits, in a tourist shop, 1959. Tufted, gray, and long on a rack with other, more luxuriant, furs; it had cost ten dollars, which I, being a child, did not have. I saw it was, profoundly and unmistakably, the same skin as the skins of the animals I'd seen in the dream, mentioned above, two or three or four years earlier and, perhaps and likely, in a book before that as well. Later though— out of an evening at a drive-in theater in 1961—I had occasion to watch an orphaned boy, my age, in a film set in Spain, being plagued by dreams that he was himself "a wolf, like in a picture book," during which time a wolf (or a dog) was "abroad" killing goats in the countryside. His adopted father put up bars on the boy's window then, he said, to "keep your nightmares away."

One thing changes every thing.

In fact, *necessity* is plural and multiple addresses—as noted above—will serve.

What, Negro?

ACKNOWLEDGMENTS

Thanks to the editors of the publications in which these poems first appeared:

Academy of American Poets' Poem-a-Day: "First Dream" and "Portland Parish/ The Blue Mountains."
Callaloo: excerpt from "Camptown."
Chicago Review: excerpt from "Camptown."
Paris Review: "Second Dream."

"Overlapping Apexes (*for Ed Roberson*)" was originally printed in *European Romantic Review* 28, no. 3 (May 4, 2017) and is reprinted by permission of the publisher (Taylor & Francis Ltd, http://www.tandfonline.com). It was also published as a pamphlet by Portable Press at Yo-Yo Labs. Special thanks to Brenda Ijima.

"Notes on Region" first appeared in *Geopoetics in Practice*, edited by Eric Magrane, Linda Russo, Sarah de Leeuw, and Craig Santos Perez (Abingdon, UK: Routledge, 2020) and is reprinted by permission of the publisher (Routledge/Taylor & Francis Group, http://www.taylorfrancis.com).

"First Dream," which appeared on the Poem-a-Day website, was published later as a poster for the Public Poetry Project of the Pennsylvania Center for the Book, a state-level affiliate of the Library of Congress Center for the Book. Special thanks to Gabeba Baderoon and Caroline Wermuth.

SOURCES

Mayer, Brantz. *Tah-gah-jute, or Logan and Captain Michael Cresap: A Discourse Delivered in Baltimore before the Maryland Historical Society on Its Sixth Anniversary, 9 May, 1851.* Baltimore, MD: J. Murphy, 1851.

Seven Dreams

Calzarette, Joe. *View from Negro Mountain (Mt. Davis highpoint) looking towards Laurel Ridge to the west.* Digital image. 2007. Accessed January 1, 2022. https://commons.wikimedia.org/wiki/File:Negro_mountain.jpg.

Cohen, Leonard. "The Bus." In *Flowers for Hitler.* Toronto: McClelland and Stewart, 1964.

Shoemaker, Henry W. *Extinct Pennsylvania Animals, Part 1: The Panther and the Wolf.* Altoona, PA: Altoona Tribune Publishing Company, 1917.

Shoemaker wrote: "Wolves singly and in pairs were tracked in the Seven Mountains during the winters of 1903, 1904 and 1905. P. F. Conser, a Millheim farmer, was working in one of his fields with his son Harry in March, 1908, when they saw a black wolf trotting along in a southerly direction, evidently headed for the Seven Mountains. This gave rise to the story that the wolves were returning to the Seven Mountains. . . . A pack of Centre County grey wolves was reduced in numbers by Samuel Askey, of Snow Shoe, who killed ninety-eight between 1820 and 1845. A pack of brown wolves hung on in the Buffalo Mountain Country, and ranged up to the White Deer Mountains until April, 1853. Famished, they attacked some dogs belonging to a raft moored at the foot of Bald Eagle Mountain, near Muncy, but most of them were shot by raftsmen. That was the last heard of the pack, which was undoubtedly the last pack in that part of Pennsylvania. . . . There was a pack of grey wolves in Blair and Cambria County, which ranged into other more southerly counties, and another pack of grey wolves in Somerset County, which inhabited Laurel Ridge."

Susquehanna River Crossing. Karthaus, PA.

The location described in "Third Dream" is the 1937 truss bridge in Karthaus, Pennsylvania, which carries state road 879 over the West Branch of the Susquehanna River; at the lip of the western end of the bridge Route 879 is crossed by the R. J. Corman Railroad, and the crossing is protected by automatic flashing lights including—for westbound traffic—a cantilever-mounted pair. Karthaus—an unincorporated community—is located on the Quehanna Plateau, a vast wild area inhabited by elk, coyotes, bobcats, fishers, pileated woodpeckers, and crows.

Tremblay-McGaw, Robin. "10th Annual Poets Theater Performances at Small Press Traffic." *X Poetics* (blog), January 30, 2011. http://xpoetics.blogspot.com/2011/01/.

Tremblay-McGaw wrote:

Lycanthropes/Entre Chien et Loup
written and directed by C. S. Giscombe
featuring Madison Hardy (as Marcella), Ryan Schaefer, George Spelvin, and Emma
    Tome. Music by Anthony Bello. Based on a true story.

From [the blog] Naked Translations: "Entre chien et loup is a multi-layered expression. It is used to describe a specific time of day, just before night, when the light is so dim you can't distinguish a dog from a wolf. However, it's not all about levels of light. It also expresses that limit between the familiar, the comfortable versus the unknown and the dangerous (or between the domestic and the wild). It is an uncertain threshold between hope and fear."

[Giscombe's] play featured excellent wolf masks and great atmosphere. Marcella, a white girl, had stories to tell, questions to ask, issues of race and gender to probe, while the wolves prowled and paced about a park-like setting (a park bench on stage). One of the wolves played a guitar and sang. . . . and there is screaming.

The Negro Mountains

Blake, William. *Songs of Innocence and Experience: Shewing the Two Contrary States of the Human Soul, 1789–1794*. Oxford: Oxford University Press, 1977.
Bracey, Christopher. "Some Thoughts on Negro Mountain." Blackprof.com, August 8, 2006.

Bracey wrote: "[A]lthough Negro Mountain's status as the highest point in the State had been confirmed by geologists, it was not officially recognized as such until 1921. In fact, locals referred to the [small plateau on Negro Mountain that rises to 3,213 feet] as just a bump on a much less politically correct and far more unpleasant name for that same mountain range. In 1921, however, the bump on Negro Mountain was designated Mount Davis, named after John N. Davis—a white settler who once owned the land—and from that day forward, Mt. Davis became known as the highest point in the State of Pennsylvania.

I'm not sure which is more tragic: the vulgar richness and symbolism of incomplete humanity exemplified by a mountain range impersonally named after a fiercely loyal

Negro slave-cum-soldier who gave his life doing battle against the Indians on behalf of his white master, or the liberal Quaker State's steadfast refusal to recognize a monument to Negro bravery (however crass and unsophisticated it appears by today's standards) until it had been literally white-washed of its connection to America's racial history."

Diddley, Bo. "Who Do You Love?" Checker Records, 1956.

cf. Hoover. Comment on "Talk like a gangsta night, dawgs." *TalkBass.com (blog)*, February 25, 2010. https://www.talkbass.com/threads/talk-like-a-gangsta-night-dawgs.632171/page-3. Hoover wrote: "One of my favorite poems, written a decade or two before rap music became an industry and nearly a half century before 'gangsta' became common lingo, by H. Rap Brown."

Giscombe, Daisy Smith. Conversation(s) with the author. Dayton, OH, circa 1966.

Leopold, Aldo. "Thinking Like a Mountain." In *A Sand County Almanac: And Sketches Here and There*. Oxford: Oxford University Press, 1949.

Leopold wrote: "Only the ineducable tyro can fail to sense the presence or absence of wolves, or the fact that mountains have a secret opinion about them."

Meyersdale Republican. Section D-Industry. "Mount Davis, Pennsylvania." September 16, 1950. Posted to Salisbury Pennsylvania Historical Website. Accessed January 1, 2022. http://www.salisburypa.com/MtDavis.html.

Italics added; note the contradiction in the Fergus note below:

"Christening of Mt. Davis Big Event for Roof Garden of Pennsylvania in 1921"

It was Governor Martin G. Brumbaugh who, during one of his visits to the country (about 1914), first referred to Somerset County as the "Roof Garden of Pennsylvania." In 1921 the U. S. Geological Survey established the fact the crest of Negro Mountain is 3,213 feet above sea level. This survey officially took away from Bedford County's Blue Knob (el. 3,136) the honor of being the highest point in Pennsylvania. Soon after the altitude of the highest point was announced, the Alpine Club of Pennsylvania decided to visit it. Under the leadership of Col. Henry W. Shoemaker, well known historian of Pennsylvania folk lore and publisher of the Altoona Tribune, the Alpine club planned a pilgrimage to the summit to assist in naming it and dedicating it as the highest point. Through the efforts of the Meyersdale Chamber of Commerce and the publicity given the event by THE REPUBLICAN, June 18, 1921 became a red letter day in the history of Somerset County. . . .

A party of hikers from Somerset went by early train to Markleton and from there hiked it to the Peck farm to join the ascent of the Alpine Club. For several preceding weeks there had been public discussion about an appropriate name for the highest point in Pennsylvania. The Alpine Club had suggested Mount Freedom among others, and the Alpiners were a little disappointed when they got here and found that the name Mt. Davis had been decided upon locally.

The name of Mt. Davis was the appropriate choice of the County Commissioners, in honor of the late John N. Davis, who was a pioneer farmer in the Negro Mountain district, land surveyor and educator. He owned the tract on top of Negro Mountain. The Davis brothers, sons of the pioneer[,] erected a flag pole at the high point to be used at the ceremony.

Shakespeare, William. *As You Like It*. New York: Washington Square Press, 1997.

Sun Ra and His Arkestra. "Make Another Mistake." *Somewhere Over the Rainbow*. Saturn Records, 1977.

Camptown

Cassidy, Frederic G., and Joan Houston Hall, eds. *Dictionary of American Regional English*. Vol 2. Cambridge, MA: Belknap Press, 1991.

The editors wrote of "evil": "(B) Senses (1) Of persons: disagreeable, unpleasant, contentious. Chiefly among Black speakers. . . . Evil QuGG35b, 'Because she couldn't go, she's been _____ all day.'"

Greene, Graham. *The Ministry of Fear*. New York: Penguin Classics, 2005.

"Garde Pitti Mulet Là (Mr. Banjo)" (song). Lyrics reprinted in Jessica Foy Long. "Forgotten Voices: An Examination of Black Louisiana Creole Folk Song through the Works of Maud Cuney-Hare and Camille Nickerson." Handout for paper presented at the 55th National Conference of the National Association of Teachers of Singing, June 23, 2018. https://www.nats.org/_Library/Las_Vegas_2018_presentations_handouts/NATS-Forgotten_Voices_Handout_-JLong.pdf.

"Saab Makes a Well-Built Swede for Every Need" (sales booklet). Södertälje and Trollhättan, Sweden: Saab-Scania Automotive Group, 1970.

Stevens, Wallace. "Two at Norfolk." In *Harmonium*. New York: Alfred A. Knopf, 1923. Posted online at Poetry Nook: Poetry for Every Occasion. Accessed January 13, 2022. https://www.poetrynook.com/poem/two-norfolk.

Overlapping Apexes

Blake, William. "Proverbs of Hell." 1793. Posted online at Poets.org. Accessed May 13, 2020. https://poets.org/poem/proverbs-hell.

Brooks, Gwendolyn. *Blacks*. Chicago: Third World Press, 1994.

Cassidy, Frederic G., and R. G. Le Page. *Dictionary of Jamaican English*. 2nd ed. Cambridge: Cambridge University Press, 2009.

The editors wrote: "Buff (House) sb obs ; evid < *above* (cf *bou*) + *house* . (Also St. Kitts, Antigua, etc.). Buff: the 'great house' or European residence on a property. . . . Obsolete, and only traced in place-names, e.g. Buff Bay."

"Ed Roberson." Special section, *Callaloo* 33, no. 3 (Summer 2010).

Greene, Graham. *It's a Battlefield*. London: Penguin, 1977.

Hayden, Robert. *Collected Poems.* Rev. ed. New York: Liveright, 2013.

Ledbetter, Huddie William (aka Lead Belly). "Midnight Special." *The Midnight Special and Other Southern Prison Songs.* Victor Records, 1940.

McClure, Michael. *Jaguar Skies.* New York: New Directions, 1975.

Nugent, Maria. *Lady Nugent's Journal of Her Residence in Jamaica from 1801 to 1805.* Kingston, Jamaica: University Press of the West Indies, 2003.

"Return of the Charles-Town Maroons. 1st November 1831." Jamaican Family Search, Genealogy Research Library. Accessed June 18, 2022. http://www.jamaicanfamilysearch.com/Members/MaroonsCharlesTown1831.htm.

Scarborough, Dorothy. *On the Trail of Negro Folksongs.* Cambridge, MA: Harvard University Press, 1925.

Stedman, John Gabriel. *Narrative of Five Years Expedition against the Revolted Negroes of Surinam: Transcribed for the First Time from the Original 1790 Manuscript.* New York: Open Road Media, 2016.

Stratton, Jon. "The Trouble with Zombies: Bare Life, *Muselmänner* and Displaced People." *Somatechnics* 1, no. 1 (March 2011).

"Symbolism in France." A World History of Art. Accessed May 3, 2012. http://www.all-art.org/symbolism/rousseau07.htm.

Westfall, Scottie. "Teddy Roosevelt and the Supposed Maned Wolf/Dog Hybrids." *Natural History with Scottie Westfall* (blog), July 25, 2011. https://retrieverman.wordpress.com/2011/07/25/teddy-roosevelt-and-the-supposed-maned-wolfdog-hybrids/.

Woman who sold copies of *Street Spirit* in front of the Shattuck Cinemas of Berkeley. Conversation with the author. Berkeley, CA, 2017.

Notes on Region

Atwood, Margaret. *The Journals of Susanna Moodie.* New York: Oxford University Press, 1970.

Bedell, John. "Thomas Cresap and Maryland's Colonial Frontier." Archaeology Program, National Park Service, US Department of Interior. Accessed December 1, 2022. https://www.nps.gov/archeology/sites/npsites/cnocresap.htm.

Benois, Nicola, David Brownell, and Nancy Conkle. *Peter and the Wolf.* Santa Barbara, CA: Bellerophon, 2002.

Browning, Meshach. *Forty-Four Years of the Life of a Hunter: Being Reminiscences of Meshach Browning, a Maryland Hunter.* Philadelphia: J. B. Lippincott, 1859.

Brusca, Frank. "U.S. Route 40: Negro Mountain." Route40.net. Updated February 27, 2014. http://www.route40.net/page.asp?n=11119.

Calvert, J. B. "The Llano Estacado." Iron, May 22, 2001. Accessed June 25, 2018. https://mysite.du.edu/~jcalvert/geol/llano.html.

Charles, Prospere. Conversation with the author. Charles Town, Portland Parish, Jamaica, 2016.

Corbett, Bob, and Jan Chatland. Accessed June 26, 2018. "Descriptions of Various Loa of Voodoo." Haiti (page), Bob Corbett, Webster University. http://faculty.webster.edu/corbetre/haiti/voodoo/biglist.htm.

Cresap, Thomas. "Letter." *Pennsylvania Gazette,* June 6, 1756.

Cresap Society. "Full Text of 'The Cresap Society Meeting at Cumberland, Md. June 14th, 1919.'" Internet Archive. Accessed June 26, 2018. https://archive.org/stream/cresapsociety meeoocres/cresapsocietymeeoocres_djvu.txt.

David Rumsey Historical Map Collection. Accessed June 25, 2018. https://www.davidrumsey .com/.

Eisenberg, Cristina. *The Carnivore Way*. Washington, DC: Island Press, 2015.

Elysee, M., *COUCOU Magazine*. May 2018. https://coucoumagazine.net/tag/books/.

Fergus, Charles. *Natural Pennsylvania: Exploring the State Forest Natural Areas*. 1917 (?). Mechanicsburg, PA: Stackpole Books, 2001.

> Fergus wrote: "The following . . . is from a speech given by Col. Henry Shoemaker, Pennsylvania newspaperman, booster, and demihistorian, in the early twentieth century: 'Negro Mountain was one of the first peaks in Pennsylvania to receive a definite name, way back in 1755. . . . Colonel Thomas Cresap, famed as the instigator of the so-called Cresap's war over the border between Pennsylvania and Maryland, was marching to join General Braddock, accompanied by a group of his personal retainers and servants. They bivouacked for the night at the foot of an enormous mountain [where] they were surprised by hostile Indians. . . . The only person killed was the colonel's favorite Negro body servant, a black of colossal proportions. The Indians were driven off, and the body of the unfortunate Negro dropped down in a deep crevice of the rocks in a shoulder of the mountain, and the party resumed its way.' According to Shoemaker, bigotry reared its ugly head soon after Negro Mountain was found to be the highest point in the state, when some people wanted to change its name; but a group called the Pennsylvania Alpine Club stood firmly for the traditional moniker, and it was kept."

> [Author's note: General Braddock died at the Battle of the Monongahela in July 1755. Colonel Cresap would not have been marching to join him in 1756, the year during which the "incident" detailed in Cresap's *Pennsylvania Gazette* letter took place.]

Fisher, Terence, dir. *The Curse of the Werewolf*. Bray, UK: Hammer Film Productions, 1961.

Giscombe, C. S. *Prairie Style*. Champaign-Urbana, IL: Dalkey Archive, 2008.

> Giscombe wrote: "On the popular Black River tours [in southern Jamaica] crocodiles approach the boat when the pilot calls them. Paradise is full of tremendous images. . . . 'This is his house, I'll see if he's home,' the pilot would say. And then would shout the name of the crocodile."

"Henri Rousseau *Negro Attacked by a Jaguar* Painting." Best Paintings for Sale. Accessed June 25, 2018. http://bestpaintingsforsale.com/painting/negro_attacked_by_a_jaguar-10273.html.

Herrero, Stephen. *Bear Attacks: Their Causes and Avoidance*. Lanham, MD: Rowman and Littlefield, 2018.

Hoffmeister, Donald F., and Herbert S. Zim. *Mammals: A Fully Illustrated, Authoritative and Easy-to-Use Guide*. New York: St. Martin's Press, 2014.

Hurston, Zora Neale. *Their Eyes Were Watching God*. Champaign-Urbana, IL: University of Illinois Press, 1991.

Irby, Kenneth. *The Intent On.* Berkeley, CA: North Atlantic Books, 2009.

Johnson, Douglas. "How Rivers Cut Gateways Through Mountains." *Scientific Monthly* 38, no. 2 (February 1934).

Leopold, Aldo. "Thinking Like a Mountain." In *A Sand County Almanac: And Sketches Here and There.* Oxford: Oxford University Press, 1949.

Mars, Florence. *Witness in Philadelphia.* Baton Rouge, LA: LSU Press, 1989.

Matheson, Richard. *I Am Legend.* New York: Tor Books, 2007.

Melville, Herman. *Moby-Dick.* New York: Dover Thrift Editions, 2003.

Muehleisen, Susanne, and Bettina Migge. *Politeness and Face in Caribbean Creoles.* Amsterdam: John Benjamins Publishing, 2005.

"Negro Mountain." Hyperleap. Accessed April 3, 2021. https://hyperleap.com/topic/Negro _Mountain.

"Negro Mountain, West Virginia [sic], USA." Discover World. 2018. https://www.discoverworld .com/United-States-of America/West-Virginia/Pendleton-County/Negro-Mountain.

"Nemacolin's Path." Encyclopedia.com (*Columbia Encyclopedia,* 6th ed.). Accessed December 1, 2022. https://www.encyclopedia.com/reference/encyclopedias-almanacs-transcripts-and -maps/nemacolins-path.

Oxford English Dictionary. https://oed.com.

Rutledge, Lynda Y., Paul J. Wilson, Cornelya F. C. Klütsch, Brent R. Patterson, and Bradley N. White. "Conservation Genomics in Perspective: A Holistic Approach to Understanding Canis Evolution in North America." *Biological Conservation* 155 (October 2012).

Shoemaker, Henry Wharton. *Addresses.* Pennsylvania: Tribune Press, 1916.

———. *Extinct Pennsylvania Animals.* Landisville, PA: Arment Biological Press, 2000.

"Somerset County, Pennsylvania." Wikipedia. Accessed June 26, 2018. https://en.wikipedia.org /wiki/Somerset_County,_Pennsylvania.

Stevenson, Mary Louise Cresap. "Colonel Thomas Cresap." *Ohio Archaeological and History Quarterly* 10, no. 1 (July 1901). https://resources.ohiohistory.org/ohj/search/display .php?page=18&ipp=20&searchterm=Array&vol=10&pages=146-164.

Summers, Montague. *The Werewolf in Lore and Legend.* New York: Courier Corporation, 2003.

Thiel, Richard P., and Adrian P. Wydeven. *Eastern Wolf* (Canis lycaon) *Status Assessment Report Covering East-Central North America, 2011.* US Fish and Wildlife Service. Accessed June 26, 2018. Fws.gov.

"treblemaker." "Thread: Nigger Mountain........." *The Value of a Nigger.* Accessed June 26, 2018. http://niggermania.net/forum/showthread.php?16711-nigger-Mountain.

VonHoldt, Bridgett M., John P. Pollinger, Dent A. Earl, James C. Knowles, Adam R. Boyko, Heidi Parker, Eli Geffen, et al. "A Genome-Wide Perspective on the Evolutionary History of Enigmatic Wolf-Like Canids." *Genome Research* 21, no. 8 (August 2011). https://www.ncbi .nlm.nih.gov/pmc/articles/PMC3149496/.

"Where Are the Staked Plains of Texas?" News Share, May 18, 2022. https://www.newsshare.in /where-are-the-staked-plains-of-texas-38858.html.